Don't Make the Mistake!

How to Start, Manage, and Protect Your Online Business

Published by
Duswalt Press
280 N. Westlake Blvd
Westlake Village, CA 91362
Suite 110
www.duswaltpress.com

Manufactured in the United States of America, or in the United Kingdom when distributed elsewhere.

Author: Stanford, DeWitt
Title of Book: Don't Make the Mistake! How To Start, Manage And Protect Your Online Business

ISBN:
Paperback: 978-1-938015-41-0
eBook: 978-1-938015-42-7

Cover design by: Joe Potter
Interior design: Scribe Inc.

Author's URL: dwstanford.com

Contents

Introduction

Don't Make the Mistake! How to Start, Manage, and Protect Your Online Business was written to provide you with the knowledge and tools needed to avoid the mistakes that can occur when you are working with a business website. It will help you understand what you should be controlling and when to hire the professionals.

Don't make the mistake of thinking that this book is going to teach you how to create or design a business website, because it is not!

There are many books out there to help you (if you decide to) create your website yourself. I truly think that subject has been covered quite well with the numerous resources available. I will, however, touch on a few things that relate to the subject that will equip you with the information needed before you start in a later chapter in this book.

This book was created to help you navigate through the decision-making process when managing, creating, and starting your business website. It doesn't matter if you are just starting your online business or if you have been in business for some time now.

One of the main reasons I decided to write this book was to help people from getting into trouble when they start out—and it can also help you if you are currently in a difficult situation.

I would like to make a point here: If you don't have a business and you are just creating a website for your family, sports teams, or any of a number of other things, the information in this book still applies! You don't have to have a business to use the information I am supplying. Everything I talk about in this book can be utilized or applied to any type of website—not just a business website.

I have focused the book toward the small business owner because I have been involved with consulting, managing, creating, and virtually every area that pertains to the online development for small business for almost two decades now. Most, if not all, of my examples

Introduction

come from actual businesses and the events that took place during the time I spent working with clients. I am using real-world examples that will hopefully help you understand the importance of the decisions that you make when managing and creating your online business. It seems that even though I've been doing this for a very long time, businesses are still making the same mistakes they did when the Internet was young . . . many years ago. The Internet has changed tremendously, but old habits are sometimes hard to break.

My goal here is to help you from getting yourself into a situation that could cost you money, and as you will see in some cases, I talk about how it could cost you your entire online business.

It really doesn't matter where you are in the development process because, at some point in time, you will be required to contact an online professional to help you in some area of your online business. It doesn't matter if the contact is a well-established web-design company, a college student, or your neighbor who works in the business. Once you have read this book, you should be equipped to ask the correct questions and handle any situation knowing how to protect yourself and your online business.

Don't worry if you are not the technical type. I will explain in detail in each chapter what you need to know so that you can communicate clearly to any web professional or organization. When you get to the heart of the matter, there are only a few technical terms that are key to the successful management of an online business. There are a few areas that are critical to understand the ownership and management. I will break down each key element into the terms that you should use when communicating with your individual, team, or company.

Finally, you should read this book completely. Even though you may understand certain aspects of online development, don't be fooled by the name of a chapter. It's very possible that you may read something that you hadn't thought about that pertains to a specific subject. This book isn't that long to begin with, so if my tips in any particular chapter are something that you already had a handle on, it would not be a big deal.

CHAPTER 1

Don't Make the Mistake: Plan for Your Business Success

Having an online business has become a common practice in the 21st century. Based on current statistics at the time this book is being written (2016), the Internet had one billion websites. Yes, *one billion* with a *B*. This shows the incredible growth of the industry. Believe it or not, according to many sources, 90 to 97 percent of all Internet business start-ups end in failure within the first six months. So why do less than 10 percent of the online businesses succeed?

This alarming failure rate exists for a number of reasons. We've all seen a business try to make it even though it never had a chance because of a bad idea or product. But the percentage with this type of failure is relatively small. This is probably due to feedback the company received before moving forward with the online business. What about the other businesses that seem to have a viable product or service? Why are so many struggling to keep an online business alive?

Many people don't know the statistical probabilities they face when they start a business online. They don't take the online business seriously enough to investigate and plan for business management and success. Many are convinced, persuaded and encouraged into moving forward with the online business before they have adequately prepared. Just because they have a product or service doesn't mean they are ready to launch an online business. Let's face it: when looking at the numbers stated above it is clear that there are a lot of people failing!

One common mistake made by prospective businesses tends to happen from the onset. The business owner wants to start asking other people or small businesses how to get a website business online. The issue arises when the people the owner is asking start giving advice before they themselves are established. This usually happens within the first year from the time they launched their online business. It's only natural because they are excited and they talk about it. They want to show it off, and because the design looks good, the word spreads.

Many of these people are quick to tell you how they started their business, especially when they are just starting out and before they have really proven successful. Within months or a year, things are not going as well as planned and issues start to arise. Sure their website was aesthetically perfect for whatever industry they were in—but that isn't enough. All that really adds up to is a good coat of paint, nice furniture, and window-dressing . . . if we were to compare it to the physical office. Don't get me wrong—the design is an important part of your online business, but it's not the most important part at the beginning.

Usually, when the failure comes, the website owner states that the issues had nothing to do with how they started their online business. The excuse is always because of some external person or business. But the fact is the owner is solely responsible because they did not take the proper steps to prevent it.

One of the biggest mistakes in the majority of these cases is that the owner didn't plan ahead of time, and as the saying goes, "If you fail to plan, then you plan to fail."

The research tells us that many people don't treat an online business with the respect and planning they would were it a brick-and-mortar (physical building) business or store. There are steps you must take before you can open a business office, store, or factory in the real world. Because everyone needs to go through the process, most of the steps are taken for granted: things like applying for a business license, filling out building lease agreements, getting office keys, and other steps that you need to perform before you can open for business. These are all the type of things that people are accustomed to doing when opening or starting a new physical location for business. So why is it that when people decide to have an online business, they disregard the need to prepare in a similar fashion? There are only a few steps that need to take place—just like opening a business or store at your local strip mall—but most online business owners skip these steps completely.

When opening a new business online, you need to take certain steps just like if you were going to open a business in a building or business center. These steps need to take place before you start your website development. Let me say it again! These steps need to take place *before* you start your online development . . . just as if you were opening an office down the street. You wouldn't have the furniture movers assigned to start moving furniture in before you signed a lease or had the keys to the building. Likewise, you need to have everything in place before you begin creating your business website.

Fortunately, there are only a couple of items that need to be accomplished, and it's much easier than the previously mentioned brick-and-mortar business action items.

I guess because the action items are very few and fairly easy to do, many business owners leave it to others to do them. I think many start-ups don't understand why it's important to keep complete control until they run into a problem.

One of the biggest mistakes a small business owner can make when starting a new website is to hire a web person or web-design company before they have done the groundwork. Many businesses think everything will be handled for them and in accordance with their desires by the web developer. One reason for this is what I like to call the "Wild West of the Internet."

The scenario usually plays out something like this: The business owner decides that they need a website for a particular business. The very first thing that they do is ask friends and acquaintances if they know of a good web-design person or company to develop the website. After they do some searching and communication, they narrow down the prospects and eventually one is picked to do the work. At this point things begin to move forward on the business development—or so the owner thinks.

Up to this point the steps that have been taken are perfectly acceptable and normal. This is generally how businesses go about getting the work done for web-development projects. Unfortunately, no planning and, more important, no foundation have been prepared for the online business first.

If the business owner has picked a developer ahead of the online foundation, this is the time when the business owner can lose control of the online business. If they haven't done the appropriate steps ahead of time, they won't have control. Let me put it this way: In this scenario, do you see the business owner finding a location for the business or getting keys to the building? No! But the business owner went ahead and hired people to start working. Now the website developer will contact the business owner (once hired) and ask if they can have the keys to the building, as well as other information. The business owner will say they don't have them and is not sure what to do. The developer will tell him that's OK and say, "We will handle it for you at no charge." This is when the business owner can lose control of his online business.

The entity that the business owner hired is just trying to do a job and get it done. If he can get it done quicker with tools he has access to, it's actually better for his business. He's saving money. You need to understand that the web development company wants your business, and they will do anything to get you as a client. Back to the Wild West of the Internet: The web-development business is very competitive, and there are tens of thousands of these companies promising you the world to get your business. So when the development is started and the business owner has not done the tasks, the development company will offer to do it for you. They will offer it because it is simple and they know how to do it. And furthermore, it gives them the opportunity to control your business future because they will own the access (keys to the building).

From this point, the owner will need to totally rely on the development company or individual. Anything that needs to be done will have to go through this development company or person. This can include domain name registration, hosting, website creation, design, and all other aspects connected with the requirements of the online business.

Think about the scenario I described: The problem here isn't the web design company. The issue is that the business owner who contacted the web company didn't perform the proper actions beforehand. This should never be the case. Who has the most to lose? The company that was hired has nothing to lose and frequently has much to gain. Say the owner needs a few things changed six months or a year after the website was completed. Who is the first person the owner will contact? If the owner decides to go with another web designer, they will need to get the information from the original design firm. Issues usually start to appear because the original design firm doesn't want to lose money to someone else. Remember, they are in complete control and the business owner has to deal with this situation now instead of running the business.

I've seen examples like this happen too many times over the years. This example is not the worst-case scenario . . . it's more like the typical scenario.

This book is full of real-life examples of what can happen when these few tasks are skipped at the beginning of the creation of a business website. Here is the good news: because you are reading this book, you will be able to avoid these mistakes.

As I stated earlier, my goal is to educate you so that you can make the best decision when dealing with the issues during this process. If you read this book, you will be in complete control of your business website and not at the mercy of others.

CHAPTER 2

Know How to Communicate Using the Business Tools

In the first chapter, I talked a lot about "steps" that need to be taken at the very beginning before you actually start your online development. These steps cannot be completed until you have a basic understanding of the tools required to complete these steps.

When people start a business, they do research about the type of business and about the competition. This is a basic move that everyone makes when starting and planning for business success. During this process, they will consider the tools that may be needed to make their business function correctly. Along these same lines, we need to look at the tools that are needed for an online business too.

Some of these tools may be familiar or they may be completely foreign to you. It doesn't matter because I will explain what you need to know to manage your online business. Most Internet professionals use acronyms for the names. This is a very common practice within the Internet world. There are a vast number of acronyms associated with many industries in our daily lives! One source I found stated that there are more than four million acronyms and abbreviations for all the different industries. This number includes technical, medical, business, and other industries. With all that data being thrown at us, it's no wonder many people don't pay attention unless it's absolutely necessary—let alone try to find out what they mean or how to use them.

The same thing can be said about some of the simplest tools that we use every day. Many people (whether they are running a business or not) only learn a part of the process for a particular tool. This makes complete sense because most people are only going to learn what they need to accomplish a task.

I will give you a simple example. Let's talk about a tool virtually everyone uses every day: e-mail! Certainly, the majority of people will think they know everything there is to know about e-mail . . . after all, they use it every day! What if today you couldn't get your e-mail? Would you know what to do? Do you know what type of e-mail you have? Did you take the necessary precautions in case this happened? Do you know how to recover your e-mail? The fact is, there is more to e-mail than most people know or care to worry about. They just expect it to be there, and the only time that they care to understand more about it is when they have a problem. Once the problem arises, their full attention is placed on the issue and they want to find out what they can do to resolve it.

In reality, the web-based acronyms needed that could pertain to an online business are much fewer than the millions stated earlier. I would say there are around fifty acronyms that could possibly cross your desk at some point in time if you wanted to be able to converse completely with any development organization. But don't worry, I'm not suggesting or expecting that you should learn all fifty, and it's not necessary. It would be nice if you have the time, but for a business website owner, it's not necessary. Only a few are required when owning and managing your online business.

What if I told you that all you really need to learn is five Internet acronyms? You read correctly—only five! I'm going to teach you the five acronyms along with three main tools that will allow you to be successful, secure, and in control while running your online business. I think it's safe to say that most of you probably have heard of most of these already. I'm including all eight because I want to make sure that I equipped you with the knowledge needed so that you can communicate with confidence while managing your online business.

Here are the eight basic tools that you should understand:

URL
Uniform resource locator. This is used to refer to the address of a web page—for example, www.mywebsite.com.

FTP
File transfer protocol. This is the system you use for uploading files to a website. Basically, it's the

way to upload pictures, documents, webpages, and any other items you want on your website or server.

DNS

Domain name system. This is what links the domain name to your website (URL) address. All you really need to know is that the DNS is numbers behind URL and that you may need to be able to point it to your business website.

HTTP

Hypertext transfer protocol. Browsers use this system to download web pages and display them on-screen.

HTTPS

Hypertext transfer protocol (Secure). This is a secured version of HTTP used by many websites such as banks. It's what you want for any personal or monetary transactions on the Internet for security.

SERVER

Servers can run on any computer, including dedicated computers. Servers often provide essential services across a network, either to private users inside a large organization or to public users via the Internet.

DOMAIN NAME REGISTER
A domain name registrar is an organization or commercial entity that manages the reservation of Internet domain names.

HOSTING
Hosting is on a server. It's a place to put your website on the Internet so people can see it. It's the building that you would be leasing if your business was at a physical address.

I have more good news: knowledge of the items listed here will allow you to communicate completely with any development team, but only three are critical to the safety and security of your online business.

I do have a warning: Don't think that you have to learn everything about all eight of these tools, because some of these items could cover a book all by themselves. I have simplified everything for you. I'm going to show you the important parts of each of these tools that pertain to your business needs—and also the functions that you need to know for survival and management.

These are the types of things that business people who encounter problems didn't educate themselves on. Just because you know the name and maybe a few things about a specific item doesn't mean you know what is required and what is not. But if you do "know it all," then these topics are so short that it should be worth a few minutes to make sure . . . besides, you already purchased the book, so you might as well read it!

CHAPTER 3

What's in a Name?

If you are just starting your online business or perhaps adding another business to the Internet, the first thing you will need to do is purchase a name for your website. This website name, as you probably already know, is called a "domain name." It's the website name that your customers use when typing in the browser to connect to your website. It's used with the URL (uniform resource locator), as you learned in the last chapter.

I'm including this topic because I have had a few clients that ran into issues with the names that they owned. I want you to know there are ramifications to think about when choosing a domain name.

Important! Don't worry about matching your business name *if it's not available*!

Of course most companies would like to use their company name as their domain name. That is a perfectly acceptable idea if it's available and you can get it without paying a ransom for it!

It has become big business for companies to buy domain names and store them away, thinking that someday they'll be able to sell that domain name for a huge profit. So if your domain name is up for sale and the seller isn't trying to get rich, you could snatch it up. But if your domain name is already gone, just move forward. I will give you tips on how to pick another name, and it might work better than your company name would have.

This leads me to my next tip when creating a new domain name for your business: make the domain name unique. Nothing sets you apart from other businesses more than using a unique name. Remember, if the name you use is similar to other commonly used names, it could cause confusion.

I have another example from clients who were requesting help. They stated that their customers kept going to a competitor's website because the domain names were similar. Had the clients done some research before they registered the domain name, they would have seen that this name was very competitive and a very similar name was being used.

In another example, a lawsuit is pending because two companies are using similar names: "YOU FIT" and "FIT U." According to the suit, they are very similar trademarks in both sight and sound. In addition, both trademarks were used to market health clubs, further adding to potential confusion. This is a great example of what to avoid if possible when picking a domain name: you must be aware of the rules that could apply to your business on the Internet.

Another key tip when picking a domain name would be making the domain name as short as possible. Let's face it, typing a long domain name is just painful. The longer the domain name, the more chances of mistakes being made during typing. Remember: the goal here is to get your customers to the correct website and making it easy for them. A good suggestion would be to take your company name and try to abbreviate it.

Whatever you decide to do—keep your options flexible. The actual domain name isn't that big of a deal for a small business website in most cases. You should be able to come up with something similar to your business name without much effort.

When looking for a domain name, you will want to use the dot-com extension. There are a couple of reasons I say this, but by far the most important reason is that people (when typing in a name) almost always put in the dot-com first out of habit. So if you don't own a dot-com and the person types in the name using the dot-com, the user will go to another business website. If it's a competitor of yours, then they just got your business! If they didn't get your business, you may have just lost prospective clients because they don't know how to find you!

Other good reasons to use the dot-com, according to many experts, are brand and search ranking benefits. This book isn't going to get into the search engine topics, but just know that a business is usually associated with the dot-com and you can use the ideas I provide here to help you create one.

When a new business starts, many times the owner will check to see if the business name has a trademark associated with it. It's a good idea and something to consider doing when searching for a domain name or your website.

One of my clients loved college sports and decided to make an online sports gaming site for fun, thinking they would turn it into a business someday. They used the website regularly with a group of friends. I'm not going to name the actual sport or website because of privacy issues. A few years later, the clients wanted to turn this website into a business—which had been the original intent. They spent a lot of money developing the website into a business and getting it ready for the big launch. As it turned out, the name they used for the website had been trademarked by a major television network. The last I heard, both parties were in litigation over the rights to use the domain name. Now remember, they had owned the website for a few years and used it regularly, but the fact was that they didn't check the trademark.

My point here is to not overlook this issue. It is very easy to check and see if someone has trademarked a name.

Trademark and copyright registrations are both issued by the federal government and protect two distinct types of intellectual property.

A trademark protects names, terms, and symbols that are used to identify the source of goods and/or services on the market. In other words, a trademark allows the consumer to distinguish one company's offerings from another's. Trademarks include brand names such as "Coca-Cola" and images such as Nike's famous "swoosh." As the owner of a federally registered trademark, you can sue for trademark infringement in federal court and prevent the importation of foreign goods that display your trademark.

A copyright protects original creative works such as books, movies, songs, paintings, photographs, web content, and choreography. As the owner of a federally registered copyright, you can control how your work is reproduced, distributed, and presented publicly, and you can sue infringers in federal court and prevent others from importing infringing goods.

CHAPTER 4

Registration Is Your Best Friend

In this chapter, you will see the importance of *registering your domain name* for your website. Please take a few minutes to read this chapter . . . you might save yourself some unneeded anguish.

It is my belief that this chapter is one of the most important in the entire book. I say this because of the consequences of not taking this simple step. Many business owners underestimate the importance of this simple but required process to owning your business website.

Just in case you didn't read Chapter 3 and you are confused, please read Chapter 3 so you understand about domain names. You can't have a website without a domain name, and that name needs to be registered. I'm amazed at how many owners don't take the time to register it themselves.

I have had countless businesses contact me over the years when they are having an issue with their web designer, developer, or hosting company. They want to know if I can help them with their dilemma. When asked, "What seems to be the problem?" most of the time the answer is that the business owner can't get control of their website.

During my practice when talking with the prospective business, I always ask, "Do you own your website name (domain name)?" Almost every time the answer is "Yes, of course we own it!" Later when I start checking the domain records, I discover that they don't "own" the name. The business owner thinks they own the domain name, but because they let the web professional take care it when they offered to, it was put in another name. When I contact the business owner and inform them of the situation, many times the owner replies, "Well it's my business and I own it." They don't understand that legally the website domain name doesn't belong to them.

A perfect example of this is a client I had recently who contacted me because they had a dispute with their web developer. They were told that I might be able help them get things resolved. The business owner just wanted to get things under control so they could move forward with their business plans. The client had a successful online business, and after a three-year relationship with the web developer, the owner started having issues with him. The developer had been hired from the very beginning to create the business website and, as it turns out, had complete control. He had maintained all the changes for the business website during this time. When the client contacted me, the developer had stopped listening to the owner's request for changes. This just happened to be at the same time that the owner had hired another professional to help with the website marketing and website changes.

The old developer didn't like the fact that someone else was getting involved and probably was insecure about losing the business. So instead of listening and doing what was requested, he started giving advice and refusing to make the requested website changes from the client. Unfortunately, this particular dispute was heading into legal action among accusations from both sides. When push came to shove, the web developer threatened to shut down the owner's online business. You see, the client wasn't in control because they gave up the control at the beginning, and they were at the complete mercy of the website developer.

The above story is just one example of a business making the mistake of not registering its own website domain name. Think about it: would you allow a stranger to go fill out your paperwork for your business license, insurance papers, or other business documents and put it in their name? Of course not, these processes go to the very heart of who owns or runs the company. When you allow a developer to register your domain name, this is exactly what you're doing.

Ultimately I did help the client get the website name registered under their business name and contacts. All this could have been avoided had the clients taken the one simple step of registering the website name themselves. Unfortunately, not every business gets away so easily without going to court or having to pay large sums of money for what was rightfully theirs. Please believe me when I say this type of example happens all too often in varying degrees. Do not consider this an isolated incident, because it is not.

If you are one of the many small businesses out there that does not have your business website name under your control, and you have access to your website or you are still in a good working relationship with the person who has control, then you should consider yourself one of the lucky ones. You should contact them as soon as possible and rectify the situation. The process is easy, and in the following paragraphs, I will explain how easy it is to register your domain name.

Now you should have a clear understanding that you should always register your domain name under your account. You also need to keep your domain name registration separate from other activities within the account. This will allow you to keep your domain license secure and under your control. There is no reason whatsoever why any web developer, programmer, or designer would need access to your domain name information.

Once you read this book and understand how to keep things separate in your account, you will have nothing to worry about. Had the business owner above just done this simple thing, he would have never had any problems or needed to contact me. The web developer could have run things without any contact with the owner if needed, but the owner would always have had the access to cut off the developer at any time.

Many businesses make the mistake of having their hosting and domain registration together under the same account. I understand why: because people don't want to have multiple accounts. Unless you pick a vendor that allows you to create other user accounts or subusers for access, it would be better for you to have two accounts and have complete control. It should be obvious to you now that if you don't do this, you are risking your business to exposure and possibly losing control of your business website.

At some point when owning a business website, a web professional is going to need access to your hosting account or other development areas. When they access that account, they will have full control of your domain name also—if you didn't make it separate. If you don't follow my advice, the developer will have no choice but to log in as "you," and that will create the problem, so don't make this potentially fatal mistake.

One thing you need to know to manage your domain name is the term "DNS" and how to change it. The term DNS doesn't mean "don't know squat!" The term DNS stands for domain name system.

Understanding this simple term and how you need to use it is what allows you as the domain name registrant and owner complete freedom from giving out your access. It is the key that a web developer will use to get your login information. If you don't know what it is or how to change it, you will need to give out your domain name account information. This would be like giving out your bank account username and password—in most cases your credit card information will be showing in your DNS administration area as well. So not only are you potentially giving your website access away but your payment information also.

In my experience, I have found that out of every twenty-five small business owners, only four or five will know what DNS is and what you are about to learn. If they do understand what DNS stands for, they don't understand its use for their website.

I can go into a long-winded technical dissertation about how the domain name system was created and how it affects IP addresses and so on, but you are a business owner and you don't really care about that. All you want to be able to do is to control your destiny and make changes when needed.

Let me sum this up by saying that after you register your domain name, there will be only two things you will ever need to do in this account. One will be to update your personal information from time to time. The only other thing you will ever need to do is change the DNS setting when you move your website or start with a new hosting company.

The DNS is used to point to your website location. It is just a pointer to your website . . . that's it!

Okay, so now you're saying to yourself, "This all sounds good, but I don't know how to change my DNS." Let me address that issue: You will be given a DNS from your new hosting company. They will give it to you when you sign up or will instruct you where to look to find it in your administration panel.

All domains have at least two DNS servers, so you will see two domain name servers. Here is an example of a name server format:

NS1.EXAMPLE.COM and NS2.EXAMPLE.COM

If for some reason you are using a third-party service or a web developer who is setting the hosting up for you, they may ask for your login to your domain name account. They will tell you that they need to get into your account to set the DNS. It is important you tell them no. You then tell them that you just need the DNS from them and you will make the changes to point it to the website. Once you get the information, all you need to do is log in and find the DNS located in your account area. Now you change the DNS to the new information they supplied.

If you still don't feel comfortable making the changes, I have the answer to your problem! The domain registrar is now a part of your business team. When you pick the service, make sure they have the support to help you. Many of the companies will make the change for you, and all you need to do is give them the information that you received.

Now that you understand the terminology and know what DNS is used for, you are equipped to communicate your needs. If you use a reputable domain registration company, they will help you and even make the changes for you. Ah yes! How important the team member—or if you prefer, another business partner—can be.

A good registrar will have the following characteristics:

- An established reputation with many users (Godaddy.com is a good example with millions of customers)
- No hidden fees (such as a fee for transferring a domain out to another registrar)
- Comprehensive administration capabilities (for nameserver, mail, WHOIS, etc. settings)
- Reasonably priced registration fees
- Accreditation by a governing body (such as ICANN)

As a smart business professional, you are going to make sure that you use a company that services your needs. The key here once again is customer support or team support. Are you starting to get the idea? You want to pick a domain company that you can call and have them make the DNS changes for you. It is fast and easy because you understand what you want done. This doesn't mean you actually know how to do it, but you do know how to tell them what you want them to do.

Let's review what you have learned in this chapter. We have discussed a few very important items for your online business security: Register your domain name.

Make sure you pick a reputable domain register company when you register your domain name. Make changes to your DNS yourself or have the domain register customer support help make the changes. Don't hand out your domain register account information to any outside resource, including web development companies.

CHAPTER 5

Up in the Clouds

So what is hosting really? Let me explain briefly without all the technical jibber-jabber. Basically a hosting server is a type of computer that runs twenty-four hours a day and seven days a week. When you are surfing the web at any time (even if it's the middle of the night), everything you see is on these servers (i.e., more powerful computers). The fact is, you could purchase a desktop computer or use your current computer and host your website.

You can also purchase a special computer that is made just for hosting, and the name for this type of computer is . . . you guessed it, a "server." You would, of course, need to keep your computer running all the time and constantly be connected to the Internet. If you didn't keep it running all the time, when you turned your computer off your website would be unavailable, and that would create issues for your business because nobody could find your business information.

There is a whole list of reasons you really don't want to host using your home computer nowadays. I think the biggest deterrents are security vulnerabilities and cyberattacks. This is because if you use a home computer, you are opening it to the general public to access it. Anyone with the knowledge could hack into your website and your server. This literally means you are opening your computer up to the whole World Wide Web and all the unscrupulous individuals that would want to cause harm. This is where the hosting companies come into play as your partners in business.

Most servers that you would use today are very different from your common computer. They are built and managed by companies to handle thousands of websites. They have special security measures to protect your website because of all the online threats that have arisen these days.

Another very important service coming from the hosting companies is that almost every hosting company guarantees 99 percent uptime. This means your website will be able to be seen at least 99 percent of the time. If it ever goes down, the odds are that you wouldn't even know it. The big hosting companies use data centers with hundreds of machines and employees monitoring them twenty-four hours a day. If a problem arises, they either fix the issue or switch you over to another machine so that your website can be viewed at all times.

Okay, now that you've let me explain the rudimentary basics of what a hosting environment is in the simplest form, let me explain the way most—if not all—small businesses host a website and the types of hosting that are offered. Again, I'm not going to try to explain every complicated setup. I'm going to talk about the most common setups for a small business or personal website.

The following are the types of hosting that are offered:

Free Hosting

This type of hosting can be a good start for a personal or hobby website. Is not recommended for businesses because they always require advertising banners to be automatically displayed on your website. As a business, you need to show professionalism and you never know if your competitor's advertisement will be seen on your website if you choose this option.

Shared Hosting

The shared hosting environment is probably the most frequently used for small businesses. Because your website and other business websites are sharing the same server, it is less expensive than the dedicated hosting option.

Dedicated Hosting

Dedicated hosting means you have a complete server to yourself or your business.

Colocated Hosting

In this type of hosting, you purchase your server and manage it yourself, but it is housed in a web hosting facility. This would mainly be used when starting a small hosting or other technical company.

Now that you have an understanding of the basics of hosting and hosting environments, you need to plan what you think would be best for your business. At the start of any business, the expense is always a big issue and needs to be part of the equation. But there are other factors that may need to be weighed as well that we will discuss.

Because there are so many different types of businesses, I cannot tell you what you need when you start your online business. You need to look at the big picture. This process is no different from the one you used when looking at your business plan and estimating the business cost and manpower for your company.

You need to take into consideration what your basic needs are at the beginning and include short-term future growth. I have found that the best way to do this is to step back and look at your business goals. By looking at your business goals and plans, you should be able to decipher your hosting needs easily and quickly.

Ask yourself, "How is my online business going to function?" and "What do I need to complete the task?"

If you remember, at the beginning of this chapter I stated that the hosting company was your partner. I might have been better off stating that they are more like a team member rather than a partner. Any way you want to look at it, you need to see them as a part of your business.

I really don't understand why businesses take this process so lightly when they need a website. They let someone else pick the hosting for them. When they get into trouble, the damage is done and it's too late.

The hosting of your online business is the same as your office building or storefront. It's very important to have access to it at all times! Would you let someone else pick where your store was going to be located? I know that sounds like a silly question, so why would you let someone pick the place where your business is put on the Internet? This all goes back to taking control of your business and staying in control. You need to make sure that you can function at all times and can keep control of your business.

Because hosting is such a valuable part of your business, you need to think of it as a division of your company. Just like any major corporation, you will have a division that is hosting your company website or websites. It is important to remember that you will need to be able to communicate with your other division— and in this case the communication will be with the hosting company. So when you're picking a hosting company to be part of your company, make sure that they have open communication, acceptable hours, and all the requirements your company needs. What I'm talking about here is called customer support! This is another area you need to take into consideration when selecting and budgeting for your hosting provider. If you select a hosting provider based strictly on the most inexpensive cost, make sure that you can live with the variables that are associated with a lower hosting expense.

Here is another real-life example I like to call "one week of hell."

I had a client whose personal website was used as an informational website to support a book. The website had information about the author and a few comments with a blog. Although he did have a link on this website to purchase his book, he did not promote this website and it didn't really matter if the website had a small issue from time to time. The author's book was promoted and available to purchase on the other third-party websites.

He didn't want to spend a lot of money on hosting for this website, so he chose a very inexpensive hosting provider with a basic plan that included e-mail.

Well, one Friday he wasn't receiving any e-mails from any websites or friends. The first time this happened, he thought something was wrong with his computer, but after a day of investigation and much agony, his computer was found to be fine. On the second day, he decided to contact the hosting company to find out what the issue was. The problem was simple—he couldn't send e-mail because it wasn't working! This particular company did not have phone support unless you paid a premium, and he had decided not to pay it when he signed up for the service. It took another few days before he could contact the hosting company and get a reply. The reply came after he had started receiving his e-mail again . . . of course. This happened a few times before he decided to move to a different hosting provider with better support.

So as you can see, the hosting provider in this example seems to work fine for the author's website, but when the author decided to use the e-mail service and it had the same type of issues, it wasn't acceptable.

Understand what you are getting into when someone offers to host your business. You need to ask the right questions: What are the customer support hours? Is there phone support, or is it just e-mail? Is there FTP access and are there any restrictions to that access?

You need to know what your online business minimum requirements will be and what the hosting company will allow.

CHAPTER 6

Don't Put the Cart before the Horse

If your business involves sales of any kind, you will probably need to use some type of e-commerce or shopping cart; otherwise what would the point be of having your business website if you didn't allow the customer to purchase your product or service? As with anything else, there are some exceptions when you won't be needing this type of service. One example would be if you were going to use your website for advertising purposes only. Another example would be if in your business, you think money would not exchange hands without a physical meeting. For the most part, now almost every industry that I've looked at has a way to transact money online, even if it's just for a deposit of some kind . . . heck, even my doctor allows payment online!

In the early years, a potential customer couldn't purchase anything directly on the Internet without contacting the business first. Typically the prospective customer would call to order the product using the phone number posted on the website. The effect was very similar to a printed advertisement in a magazine or newspaper. It wasn't long before businesses were asking for ways to collect money and to communicate using other methods. It didn't take long until the shopping cart industry was born. This allowed the online business to sell the product or products using a shopping cart solution without any company (employee) interaction at all to complete the sale, which saved the company money.

With the development of the e-commerce industry, it also allowed customers to order directly online without having to communicate with the business, and it made the process much easier. Another great benefit was that it helped alleviate all the human mistakes that were being made with "over-the-phone" orders.

Today you can purchase products, services, and virtually anything that someone is willing to sell on the

Internet. The e-commerce industry has become such a big part of the Internet that people now purchase items using smartphones. The fears of purchasing an item over the Internet have long since passed. Many people not only purchase items on the Internet but also do their banking and pay their bills online. With all this growth, many e-commerce companies have joined the bandwagon and offer a variety of ways for you to sell your products and services. So once again, I will use my mantra that you as the business owner "need to plan" as best you can when deciding what is best for your business when it comes to e-commerce.

When planning for this type of process, it helps to step back and look at how you conduct your particular business. This is an important step and can be easily overlooked when a business starts selling products or services online. Many of your processes and procedures may need to be integrated when conducting your business online. Some things you need to consider: Does your business have employees? Will they need access to any of the customer information, products, or accounting when products are sold? How do you handle or package your products? These types of actions need to be considered *before* you go looking for your specific e-commerce solution or provider.

Here is another real-life example of what I'm talking about. One of my clients had a very successful business website that sold colored pencils. Many years ago when they had their website developed, the developer set up a shopping cart as well as the website for their company. After spending thousands of dollars on the website, design, and the shopping cart, orders started coming in. The employees were processing the orders and shipments were being sent out on schedule. After a period of time, the business realized that the shopping cart didn't calculate the weight correctly, so they were losing money that should have been included in the product's cost. To make matters worse, the shopping cart would only price their merchandise per box shipped—not by the case. The business needed the shopping cart pricing to calculate the number of pencils or containers inside the box. This was standard procedure for the business, and they needed to function this way.

Unfortunately it was too late to start over because they had spent the money to get the online business developed. They had no recourse but to pay another developer to customize the shopping cart and to make all the changes. It ended up costing the client almost double the original cost and another few months of employee time to contact customers and fix any issues. And all of this was on top of the money they had lost as they shipped their products. The shopping cart had to be customized every time a security or other update was needed, and the client had no choice but to pay additional costs to the developer as long as they owned that software.

The above story is a perfect example of the business owner not being prepared and not planning ahead of time. They knew how they ran the business in the office, but they didn't do the research when including an e-commerce solution for the business website.

Like I said before, there are many different shopping cart vendors, e-commerce solutions, and providers, but when it comes to making a decision for your business, it basically boils down to just answering a few questions. Once you answer these questions, you will be ready to choose the vendor or product from one of the categories I have listed in this chapter. Before you can do this, you need to review the information about each general category.

Let's start with a general overview of what a shopping cart is. A shopping cart is software that is used online to select an item to purchase and then allows for payment and shipping of the item. You've seen them everywhere—all the major stores like Walmart, Target, and others use shopping carts so that customers like you and I can purchase an item from the comfort of our homes. When using a shopping cart, to most people they may all look pretty much the same, but behind the scenes there are many differences between them. Because not all shopping carts are created equal, we need to look at the major differences. Let's look at them now in general terms.

The three main categories of shopping carts are open source, fully hosted, and simple payment provider.

1. Open-Source Shopping Cart
Advantages

You have full control of the software; it is very customizable and it is inexpensive. The reason you have full control is because you have access to all the programming (open source) of the shopping cart. It is much more inexpensive compared to the other types of shopping carts. An open-source shopping cart is typically software that you purchase from a vendor for a one-time fee. You can even get open-source shopping carts for free. As I said, with the open-source shopping cart, you have full control and access to all the code and the programming within the software. In other words, you are free to make changes and modifications to customize the shopping cart to your company's needs.

Disadvantages

There are added costs for issues with software bugs, security, and upgrades, and there is limited support if you have any at all. You have all the power to customize the software, but you will need a programmer, which will be an added cost. Any issues with the software will require a technical person to perform all activities. The software needs to be installed on your website server or hosted somewhere else, and this will be an added cost as well.

2. Fully Hosted Shopping Cart
Advantages

This type of shopping cart is basically ready to go! It is already installed and hosted; you just need to sign-up and start using it. There is no need for hosting on your part because the shopping cart is completely taken care of by the vendor. The vendor includes all upgrades and security compliance issues. All hosted shopping carts should supply customer support.

Disadvantages

It is more expensive, and any customization will be limited to what the vendor offers. You have limited or no code access because of security.

3. Payment Service Providers with Add-on Buttons

PayPal and other companies like it are providers that allow the customer to process the payment. They can be used for a single product or service directly without a shopping cart. This type of e-commerce is best when you're only selling a few items. You just add a button into your existing website.

Advantages

This is an inexpensive alternative for a limited amount of items. It is easy to install on your existing website with plug-and-play–type buttons. No full shopping cart is needed! Reports, invoices, and payments are sent to your e-mail. No administration is required.

Disadvantages

It's pretty much use "as is" with limited design modifications.

There is one other thing I want to mention here: it is possible to use a combination of these three categories that I mentioned. I'm not going to get into these possibilities, although I've seen them. These types of things are not guaranteed because of the patch type of service. I would recommend that you avoid them altogether.

Now that you have some knowledge of the three major categories, I will give you a few key questions to answer that will help put you in the right direction when picking a category and then I'll give you a brief example of how each category works so you may make an informed decision.

Let's look at the different ways a business could possibly use each of the categories. This should help you narrow down or eliminate the types that do not fit your business model. It will also equip you with a game plan before you start looking for a vendor or cart. One note, I'm not going into all the specifics of every type of cart system, e-commerce, or vendor. You will need to shop around and look at products yourself after you have narrowed down which category you want to use.

Here are a few of the most basic and important questions to answer when picking a category.

1. How many products am I going to sell?

   One of the most important items to consider when deciding which solution to use is the number of products or services your online business will offer. If your business website will sell more than five hundred items, you would clearly use a different solution than a business that's going to sell one or two items.

2. What is the possible number of products within the next twelve to twenty-four months?

   You must look at your growth possibilities for the number of your products as well. If your business is currently only prepared to sell two items but you know that you will be increasing the number of products substantially over the next year, this may affect your decision on what solution to use at the beginning.

3. How many people (employees) will need to access and manage information?

When using a full shopping cart, you need to plan how much time in manpower it will take to administer the shopping cart.

4. Do I have a full-time technical person or programmer available?

This question is especially important if you are leaning toward the open-source shopping cart.

5. Do I have any special requirements?

Remember the example I gave about the pencil business and how it didn't examine the shipping requirements pertaining to boxes of pencils when shipping before it purchased the shopping cart, finding out later that it wasn't the correct shopping cart for the business? This would be a special requirement.

These five questions should give you a head start and an idea of how you need to think when developing your plan for an e-commerce solution.

If your online business requires someone other than yourself to manage or access customer information and/or accounting, you need to consider what type of administration your shopping cart software comes with. This is usually called the "back end" by most development professionals. It's the part that the customer never sees and that you use to check customer information, sales data, invoices, and payments.

Let us take the previous example of the client who sells colored pencils. They have a small office with three employees. These employees have multiple tasks and different levels of access to the shopping cart administration or back end. The owner doesn't want all the employees to have access to everything and every area of the shopping cart. So it's important to make sure when looking at a shopping cart that it has what your company needs in the back-end or administration part.

I will assume you are starting a small business and not a bigger, well-established Fortune 500 company. That being the case, I would highly recommend that you be very cautious when considering using the open-source software option, unless you are technically inclined with programming experience or have a full-time technical employee.

I understand it's very appealing to want to use an open-source shopping cart because they are inexpensive with little or no up-front cost, but in the long run, it can be much more expensive to manage the security and updates. Also, whatever money you may save at the beginning will be consumed with your valuable time. This is the time you would be spending on your business in other areas. So don't take it lightly. The open-source shopping cart could be much more costly to your business in the long run if you don't take these things into consideration.

To help you with the decision-making process, I will give you a few examples of the types of businesses and the e-commerce solutions they would use. Most of you could read the following and pick the appropriate solution.

Example 1

Let's say that you're a small business owner and you work out of either a home office or a small rented office. You do not employ more than one to three people and you fall into the category offering only one to ten products. You don't manufacture any of the items you sell to keep this example simple.

In this example, a product could be any item, such as coffee cups, paintbrushes, or toys. Also included for this example could be services instead of a product. In that case you would list that service with some sort of price, which could be a down payment, deposit, or service payment. Many businesses fall into this category, such as an author, accountant, consultant, notary, web designer, and many more. If this describes your small business, you should definitely use the payment service providers category.

Example 2

If you are a small business owner and have many more products than in Example 1, you should consider the fully hosted category. The fully hosted category will be a full shopping cart, which will help you keep your accounting and products organized. It will also allow you to have other employees help manage from the administration area. The more products you have, the more administrative duties will be required, like managing inventory levels, customer invoices, and so on.

Example 3

If you're a small business owner and are in the technology-based industry or have your own server and have a technology professional managing your systems, you definitely want to consider the open-source category, because any added cost for installation, setup, and ongoing security maintenance would already be absorbed into the salary you are paying for this individual or service.

There are many companies that offer each of the solutions we have discussed. Choosing a specific vendor or product will take some investigation on your part. Whichever solution you decide on, you are now prepared with the knowledge needed to move forward.

CHAPTER 7

When Do I Need
a Web Professional?

At some point you've completed the initial steps of acquiring a business license, locating a building, and getting keys to your office in the non-Internet world. In the online business world, this translates to the equivalent of purchasing a domain name, acquiring hosting, and setting up the web address for your Internet business.

When that part is complete, unless you're the creative type and have web design experience, you are going to need some professional help for your website setup and design. Some hosting companies supply a simple tool called a "website builder" that allows the user to pick a design, add a few pictures, and type some text.

I'm not a big fan of these because they are very limited in what they can do. But if you are and you want to take the added responsibility of designing your website, you can use this tool.

For the majority of small business owners, it is time to start the process of looking for a web professional. I have tried to put the chapters in the order of what you need before this step.

Note: Don't worry if you aren't sure of the exact order. I have included how the processes should flow and a worksheet later in this book as a guide.

The first thing I want to stress is that you need to be prepared *before* you contact a web professional. Just like I've stated many times, you need to take the appropriate planning steps so that you are ready when you decide it's time to search for a web professional. If you don't take this advice, you will once again open yourself up to major frustrations. The probability of not getting what you wanted as a final result is high.

You need to have a "complete package of information" about your business ready so you can hand it to the web professional once you contact them. This will make the quoting process much more accurate for you and help the prospective web professional. When information is missing, it doesn't get included in the development or in the cost estimate.

Note: the information I'm referring to here doesn't include the creative design of the website. If you have a design idea that's great, but you are not ready for that until you complete the information package. The information I'm speaking about is the text, pictures, and all the business details that are needed to create your business statements and profiles.

In the development world this information is called "content." As an example, when you visit a website and you want to know more about the company, you click on a link that says "About Us." On that page, you will learn about the company and maybe about employees, stock options, and so on. This is the information you need to supply to the developer. The developer or company does not know this information. They need the information supplied to them.

Only after you have supplied all the content and requirements should you move to the next phase, which is the design and development. Too many companies get excited about starting an online business and jump into the design phase of the website before they are ready with the content. What they don't understand is that the developer will need to take into consideration the amount of content you have before the design is complete. So if you start working with a web design company before you have all the content, the website might be completed before everything has been designed correctly or the way it needs to function.

Remember, the person you hired would have based their quote on the amount of time they estimate and would have scheduled the work appropriately. When you default on getting the information per the requirements, the schedule and the partnership crumbles. The website doesn't get completed the way you expected, and in many cases, it never gets completed by the initial web developer the way you had envisioned.

The developer that is hired can only look at what is submitted at the time of contact. If you as a customer find that you need to add items at the end of the project or want changes, the developer will need to add additional fees. In the web development industry, this can complicate the communication process. Most of the time the developer will have already started the work and what may seem to be a small change to you could cause the developer to change the code from the beginning. There is much more to consider than you may think when you want to add something. Remember: your business website isn't just designed artwork and graphics . . . it's programming too. They may look at the changes or additions that you requested and say it can't be done this way . . . it's too late! But they may say they can get it done in another way that will achieve the same result. What they are really saying is you need to pay for a redesign. They will tell you, "Don't worry, we will take care of it for you!" Of course the owners go along with the suggestion! Why wouldn't they? After all, they are the professionals and the owners hired them to handle this. When the project is completed, the cost has doubled or tripled. Now you have a problem . . . they can hold the design for ransom until you pay. You will likely lose your deposit if you don't use the work they created for you, and if you are on a budget, then you are stuck.

One reason this happens so often is that the web industry is very competitive, and once the work is approved, they get started immediately. They need to keep getting work and they don't want to lose a client. They will assume you know what you're doing and get started right away.

Another reason is that they are prepared to give an accurate quote at the beginning, but when changes are made the quoting process can get complicated because of the technical parts of the website. The development company might be subcontracting part of the technical requirements and when you make changes it affects this part of the job and that usually becomes costly and hard to forecast.

Now before I go any further, I want you to understand that I'm not here to bash the web design industry or other online professionals. After all, I've been associated with the online development community for many years. I started my first web design company back in 1999 and understand the process. There are indeed many superb professional companies that would be able to handle the above situation and communicate the cost differences to avoid any surprises. But there are many more that are not well equipped when it comes to these types of surprises. And believe me, my company has had to come to the rescue many times because of situations like this.

My whole point here is for you to avoid these types of situations by planning ahead. If you have everything ready for the web developer, this would mean that you have gone through the process to examine what you need on your website to start your online business.

If you haven't gone through the process, who is going to do it?

Some business owners make another mistake by starting this information process with the web developer. They are looking for feedback or suggestions on what to add for content. Please listen closely: You are the expert for your business. The web developer is the expert on taking the information and turning it into programming code and graphics. Why would you ask them what is best for your business? It is not what they are trained for, but they will gladly give their input and happily make suggestions to get the job done as fast as possible so they can get paid and move on!

There will be plenty of time for people to critique your website once you start your business. Remember, I'm only talking about the *content* here before you contact a web professional—mainly written text. Don't confuse this with the layout of the website or how the written content is viewed. After you have given the package to the web professional, they will give you feedback on the best ways to achieve your goal so people can read your information easily and with little effort.

It would help to have designs of your competition (if you like) or other examples of what you think looks good so the developer is heading in the direction you choose. Any creative thoughts and ideas can be discussed between you and the web professional at this time.

Work is required if you want to be successful with your online business. The percentage of business website failures shows that professionals are not taking the correct approach and not doing the work needed to achieve success.

CHAPTER 8

Business E-mail

I decided to add this short chapter about the basic types of e-mail because I brought the subject up in an earlier chapter and it will help if you run into issues.

We send a lot of e-mail these days—at work, at home, on our phones. But do you know what type of e-mail you are using? Keep reading to find out more about the difference between the various ways you send and receive e-mail.

Whether you use Gmail, Hotmail, Yahoo! mail, or e-mail configured on your own website, there is more to sending and receiving e-mail than it might seem.

Before I explain the different protocols used to download e-mails, let's take a few minutes to understand the simpler stuff—the difference between e-mail clients and webmail. If you've ever signed up for a Gmail, Hotmail, or other e-mail account, you have used webmail. If you work in an office and use a program like Microsoft Outlook, Windows Live Mail, or Mozilla Thunderbird to get and manage your e-mails, you're using an e-mail client.

Both webmail and e-mail clients are applications for sending and receiving e-mail, and they use similar methods for doing this.

Webmail is an application that is written to be operated over the Internet through a browser, hence the term *web*mail, usually with no downloaded applications or additional software necessary. All the work, so to speak, is done by remote servers and not on your computer. The e-mail isn't saved on your computer, instead it's on the server.

E-mail clients are programs that are installed on local machines (i.e., your computer or the computers in your office) to interact with the e-mail servers. They download the e-mail to your computer and keep the e-mail copies on your computer. All the work of sending and receiving as well as the user interface is done on your computer with the installed application, rather than by your browser with instructions from the remote server.

Remember the story I told you about when a client of mine didn't receive their e-mail for a week? It turned out that the hosting company was having issues with the server. But the client at first thought something was wrong with his computer. That's because they use an e-mail client. Once he figured out that the client (Microsoft Outlook) was working fine, he turned his attention to the hosting company that sends the e-mail to his computer.

So you have two options when using e-mail: You can have it stored on a server or downloaded to your computer. You might ask, "Why would I download my e-mail?" Many people and companies want to keep control and security of their e-mail. They don't want it stored on the web where it is possible that someone could get to it. In actuality, when you store it on the web, it is out of your control. When you download it through an e-mail client, you have the opportunity to back it up and save it.

Others prefer to keep it in the webmail so that they don't have to worry about having it on their computer. The choice is yours!

Now that you know that all e-mail is configured on servers, you should realize that when you sign up for a hosting company, most of the time e-mail is part of the package. This allows you to have an e-mail name that matches your online business name. It also allows you to configure the way you would like the e-mail to be sent to you with your hosting service: either using the webmail provided by the hosting company or sending it to your personal e-mail client.

CHAPTER 9

Time to Take Control (of Your Team)

Hopefully you have figured out by now that running and managing an online business is a team venture. No matter what type of online business you have, you won't be able to complete all the tasks by yourself without using outside resources. It doesn't matter if you have a Fortune 500 company or a small one-room office . . . you don't have a choice on this issue.

The reason for this and what makes it different from other types of businesses is that you are using the Internet. Let me remind you that even though you may own an online business, you don't own the Internet . . . no one does. The Internet is a separate entity all by itself and because of this, you must follow the procedures, rules, and regulations if you want to use it.

The fact is, as you go through the steps to secure your online business, most of you will be using multiple external resources.

The good news is these Internet resources have come a long way over the last few years and have made things easy for you to complete your actions with very little effort. Your responsibility is to pick the right partners to support you and your business.

I think it helps to think of these partners as team members. You are the owner of your online business, but you have team members to help you keep everything secure and running smoothly. When you think of it this way, you will move forward with the correct mind-set.

If you have read this book completely, you should be well aware of the hazards involved and what to look out for when it is time to move forward. You are well equipped now to handle each step that will be required with your partners or team members.

The steps were explained starting in Chapter 3 with the process of picking a domain name, along with the details needed to allow you to complete each of the actions. You were given examples to help you understand the importance of a given task and the possible consequences if it were skipped.

When it comes time to work on a specific action or step and you need to review the information, head to Chapter 10 (the last in the book); it has the list of steps with the actions needed. All you need to do is follow this list.

I would especially like you to review the information in any chapter if you are wondering why you should handle the step yourself. Here's a hint: it is the main reason I decided to write this book!

Hopefully you learned that planning is the key to the success of your online business. It's no different than any other business venture. If you want to succeed, some thought and planning needs to be put into it.

You are equipped with knowledge of the eight terms or tools that are needed to understand how to communicate with the team members.

You now know about the domain name, what it is, and some of the best practices when picking your online website address. You understand that you must register the domain name as well as pick a hosting partner that fits your business needs. If e-commerce is needed, you have the information on the types to pick from for your particular situation. Finally, you know what to do ahead of time, and when it's time to hire a web professional!

Nobody is perfect and neither is your business. You will make mistakes . . . but if you apply the items I put in this book, you will have fighting chance with your online business and will keep control of it at all times.

Your website design may not be as successful at the beginning as you thought it would be and you may need to adjust it. Your content more than likely will need to change from time to time. These types of issues will continue to evolve as your company moves forward and you tweak it for success! The important part is that you won't have any roadblocks in your way when these issues arise.

Now you have the power to take control of your business, and no one will have the power over your business except you!

The steps that you have taken will prevent any of the real-life scenarios you read about in the previous chapters from happening to you. You will have taken away the opportunity of malicious Internet business practices from affecting your business. You will have avoided the possibility of extra development costs when your company needs it the most—at the beginning. Most of all, you will make sure that you, the owner, have full control of your online business and that no one will be able to take that control away!

CHAPTER 10

Let's Put It All Together

I spent most of the time in this book educating you about the pitfalls of not completing the appropriate steps when you begin your business using the Internet. The rest of the time is used to give you an understanding of the terminology and tools that are needed so that you have the knowledge to complete the tasks with your external team members.

Now it's time to put it all together! To help you, I have included a simple list with the steps in the order in which they were explained in the book. Each of the steps has the appropriate chapter referenced in the list. This simple and easy list has checkboxes so you can easily keep track of your progress.

Don't Make the Mistake!

Let's review the four main steps that require an external team member.

1. Pick a domain name.
   You will be using an online resource (domain registration website) to check and see if the domain name you want is available.
2. Pick a registration company.
   You will need to select the company and create an account for the domain name you want.
3. Pick a hosting company.
   You will need to select the hosting company to house your website.
4. Hire a web professional to build your website.

When assembling your team members, keep in mind that you might use only one team member to complete more than one of the steps. A good example of this would be if you're using GoDaddy.com to register your domain name and then you decide to use GoDaddy.com for your hosting. In this case, the business that was picked offers both services.

Checklist Worksheet

❑ **Pick a domain name for your business website (Chapter 3)**
  - ❑ The domain doesn't need to match the business name
  - ❑ Dot-com is still important
  - ❑ Make the domain name unique
  - ❑ Check for trademark

❑ **Select a domain register for your online business (Chapter 4)**
  - ❑ Pick a reputable domain register company
  - ❑ Register your domain name
  - ❑ Never give out your account information

❑ **Select your hosting partner for your website and e-mail (Chapter 5)**
  - ❑ Know your hosting requirements
  - ❑ Pick the correct type of hosting environment for your business
  - ❑ Cost savings versus performance can affect the business

❑ **Select an e-commerce option (Chapter 6)**

    ❑ Analyze your need for sales

    ❑ Pick the category of shopping cart/e-commerce

    ❑ Review the procedures before selecting the solution

❑ **Hire a web Professional (Chapter 7)**

    ❑ Have a complete package of information ready

    ❑ Know what part of the work belongs to the web professional

www.ingramcontent.com/pod-product-compliance
Lightning Source LLC
Chambersburg PA
CBHW071500210326
41597CB00018B/2629